D1602229

WATCHMAN NEE

Worshipping the Ways of God

Living Stream Ministry
Anaheim, California

ISBN 1-57593-859-6

Living Stream Ministry
1853 W. Ball Road, Anaheim, CA 92804 USA
P. O. Box 2121, Anaheim, CA 92814 USA

97 98 99 00 01 / 9 8 7 6 5 4 3 2 1

WORSHIPPING
THE WAYS OF GOD

"And the man bowed down his head, and worshipped the Lord. And he said, Blessed be the Lord God of my master Abraham, who hath not left destitute my master of his mercy and his truth; I being in the way, the Lord led me to the house of my master's brethren" (Gen. 24:26-27).

"And it came to pass, that, when Abraham's servant heard their words, he worshipped the Lord, bowing himself to the earth. And the servant brought forth jewels of silver, and jewels of gold, and raiment, and gave them to Rebekah: he gave also to her brother and to her mother precious things" (vv. 52-53).

"And Aaron spake all the words which the Lord had spoken unto Moses, and did the signs in the sight of the people. And the people believed: and when they heard that the Lord had visited the children of Israel, and that he had looked upon their affliction, then they bowed their heads and worshipped" (Exo. 4:30-31).

"That ye shall say, It is the sacrifice of the Lord's passover, who passed over the houses of the children of Israel in Egypt, when he smote the Egyptians, and delivered our houses. And the people bowed the head and worshipped" (12:27).

"And the Lord descended in the cloud, and stood with him there, and proclaimed the name of the Lord. And the Lord passed by before him, and proclaimed, The Lord, The Lord God, merciful and gracious, longsuffering, and abundant in goodness and truth, keeping mercy for thousands, forgiving iniquity and transgression and sin, and that will by no means clear the guilty; visiting the iniquity of the fathers upon the children, and upon the children's children, unto the third and to the fourth generation. And Moses made haste, and bowed his head toward the earth, and worshipped. And he said, If now I have found grace in thy sight, O Lord, let my Lord, I pray thee, go among us; for it is a stiffnecked people; and pardon our iniquity and our sin, and take us for thine inheritance" (34:5-9).

"Now once, when Joshua was by Jericho, he lifted up his eyes and looked; and behold, there was a man standing opposite him, and His sword was drawn in His hand. And Joshua went to Him and said to Him, Are You for us or for our adversaries? And He said, Neither, but as the Captain of Jehovah's army have I now come. Then Joshua fell to the ground upon his face and worshipped. And he said to Him, What does my Lord speak to His servant?" (Josh. 5:13-14).

"And when Gideon heard the account of the dream and its interpretation, he worshipped. And he returned to the camp of Israel and said, Arise, for Jehovah has delivered the camp of Midian into your hand" (Judg. 7:15).

"It was for this child that I prayed, and Jehovah has granted me my request that I requested from Him. Therefore I, for my part, have lent him to Jehovah; all the days that he lives, he is lent to Jehovah. And he worshipped Jehovah there" (1 Sam. 1:27-28).

"And on the seventh day the child died. And David's servants were afraid to tell him that the child was dead; for they said, While the child was alive, we spoke to him, and he did not listen to our voice; how then can we tell him that the child is dead? He will do himself some harm. And David saw that his servants were whispering, and David perceived that the child was dead. And David said to his servants, Is the child dead? And they said, He is dead. Then David rose up from the ground and washed and anointed himself and changed his clothes. And he went to the house of Jehovah and worshipped. Then he went to his house; and when he requested it, they set food before him, and he ate" (2 Sam. 12:18-20).

"Then one day, when his sons and daughters were eating and drinking wine in the house of their firstborn brother, a messenger came to Job and said, The oxen were plowing, and the donkeys were feeding beside them; and the Sabeans fell upon them and took them away, and they struck the servants with the edge of the sword; and I alone have escaped to relate these things to you. While this one was still speaking, another came and said, The fire of God has fallen from heaven and has burned up the sheep and the servants and devoured them; and I alone have escaped to relate these things to you. While this one was still speaking, another came and said, The Chaldeans formed three companies and raided the camels and took them, and they struck the servants with the edge of the sword; and I alone have escaped to relate these things to you. While this one was still speaking, another came and said, Your sons and daughters were eating and drinking wine in the house of their first-born brother; and suddenly a great wind came from beyond the desert and struck the four corners of the house, so that it fell upon the young people and they died; and I alone have escaped to relate these things to you. Then Job rose up and tore his clothes and shaved his head and fell to the earth and worshipped" (Job 1:13-20).

We must deal with one matter before God. If we truly intend to be worshippers of God, it is impossible to just worship Him. I am not saying that we should not worship God. We must worship God, but please remember that a day will come when God opens our eyes to know Him as more than just our Father; we will know Him also as our God. We need to see that we are not only His children but also His bondservants. When we see this revelation and meet God as God, we immediately will worship Him. However, we should not stop there. Whenever we have a revelation of God and meet Him, the result should be that we accept His ways. The result of seeing and knowing God is that we accept God's ways.

God's holy Word shows us that we must know God and we must know His ways. God Himself can only be known by revelation, and God's ways can only be known through submission. We know God Himself through His revelation, and we know the ways of God by being willing to be dealt with and by submitting to Him.

WHAT ARE THE WAYS OF GOD?

What are the ways of God? The ways in which God deals with us are His ways. His ways entail what He wants to do. The ways of God are the choices He makes concerning us. These are the ways of God. His ways are higher than our ways (Isa. 55:9). He has His own ordinations, and there is no room for our choice. He deals with this person in this manner and with another person in that manner. His ways are what He deems best. The ways of God imply that God acts according to His desire and choice.

Many people balk at the fact that, without an unveiling of God to man, we cannot accept God's ways. We must first have revelation before we can accept God's ways. We ask, "Why did God love Jacob and not Esau?" We feel that God was not fair to Esau, and we even feel indignant about the way Esau was treated. We think that Esau was a very good man who was cheated out of everything. Jacob was the one who was bad. Yet God said, "Jacob have I loved, but Esau have I hated" (Rom. 9:13). Yet still we reason about this. Those who reason in this way have not seen God. Those who have seen Him know that He is God. God can act according to His pleasure. He does what makes Him happy. He is God. No one can tell Him how He should act. He does not need counselors or advisors. He does not need an advisory board to tell Him how to do things. He does what He pleases. These are the ways of God.

The ways of God are His choices. The ways of God are what He wants to do. He wants to do things this way, and He wants to deal with us in that way. He wants to accomplish this matter but not something else. He wants us to encounter this circumstance but not that one. These are the ways of God.

NOT STOPPING
WITH THE WORSHIP OF GOD

As we have already pointed out, when a person receives a revelation concerning God and he sees that He is God and that man is man, he only can bow down and worship. But we must not stop there because this is too abstract. We must immediately say, "God, I worship You, and I worship Your ways. I do not just worship You, I also worship Your ways." Our heart must be brought by God to the point of bowing down before Him and saying, "I see that I should not only worship You, but also what You have and what pleases You. I should worship what You choose. I should worship what You have ordained for me. I should worship what You are pleased to bring upon me. I should worship You for the things You do not want me to pursue." Brothers and sisters, it is easy to worship God while we are gathered here in the meeting because there is no price to pay. But let me repeat that all true worship comes from knowing God and receiving a revelation of God. Thank God, I know Him; therefore, I fall before Him, saying, "Everything You have done is right. You are never wrong." This is the way to accept the ways of God.

We learn to walk step by step. If we want to learn to walk before God, we will have no future unless we can learn to worship the ways of God—not just to worship God. Our entire spiritual future hinges on our ability to worship the ways of God. Thus, all who know God must be brought to the point of saying, "I worship the ways of God. I worship the things that God has ordained for me. I worship the things God has done to me. I worship God for what He is pleased to do in me. I worship God for the things He strips from me."

THE WORSHIPPERS OF GOD'S WAYS

Let us consider a few of the worshippers of God in the Old Testament to see how they worshipped God. We will see the ways of God from the examples of God's worshippers in the Old Testament.

Worshipping God
for a Prosperous Journey

The ways of God are what God wants to do in us. Our first illustration is found in Genesis 24. Recall the story in which

9

Abraham said to the servant who ruled over all that he had, "Go unto my country, and to my kindred, and take a wife unto my son Isaac" (v. 4). This was a formidable undertaking. Abraham was living in Canaan. In order to reach Mesopotamia one had to cross the Jordan River, the Euphrates River, and the stretch of desert lying between them. It was a difficult matter for a servant to go to a strange place a great distance away and persuade a young woman to accept this offer of marriage. Eliezer, however, was looking to God. Although it seemed as if he was going to the ends of the earth to seek Abraham's relatives and find a woman, he was trusting in God. The record in the Scriptures about his trip is very marvelous. It says that when he came unto Nahor, the city of Abraham, he prayed, "O Lord God of my master Abraham, I pray thee, send me good speed this day, and show kindness unto my master Abraham. Behold, I stand here by the well of water; and the daughters of the men of the city come out to draw water: and let it come to pass, that the damsel to whom I shall say, Let down thy pitcher, I pray thee, that I may drink; and she shall say, Drink, and I will give thy camels drink also: let the same be she that thou hast appointed for thy servant Isaac; and thereby shall I know that thou has showed kindness unto my master" (vv. 12-14). This prayer seems difficult to answer. But he had not even finished praying when Rebekah arrived at the well.

We all know the story here and that to the detail everything transpired as he had requested. But what if this damsel was not of Abraham's family? As we know, the type here is of Christ and the church, both being of one family. "He who sanctifies and those who are being sanctified are all of One" (Heb. 2:11). Rebekah needed to be of the same source as Isaac. What if she was of another race like Syrian or Babylonian? So Eliezer asked about her family background. Yes, she was Abraham's kin. Eliezer immediately bowed his head and worshipped the Lord (Gen. 24:23-27). Do we see? These are the ways of God. If we only will learn to acknowledge the Lord in all our paths as in Proverbs 3:6, we will be acknowledging God in His ways. If we request Him to do this and that and believe, looking trustfully to Him, then when things happen according to our requests, we will worship Him. Thus, we

11

will not worship God merely because He is God; we also worship Him for His actions. Eliezer immediately bowed his head and worshipped the Lord as if to say, "You have given grace to me. You have given grace to me as You have given grace to my master Abraham, and You have led me in the way."

Brothers and sisters, do we see what it means to worship God? It means to render all glory to Him. Giving glory to God does not mean that we meet with a situation which turns out well after prayer and then we say that we were lucky, that things fell into place at the right time, or that we did things well ourselves. One who knows and has seen God is one who can do nothing but bow down and worship when he sees God do something. Abraham's servant did not even stop to talk with Rebekah. The first thing he did was worship God. He did not feel embarrassed; he instantly bowed his head and said, "God, I worship You."

What is worship? Worship is giving glory to God when He has His way with us. Giving glory to God is worship. Have I made myself sufficiently clear? I hope that we would see the connection between

12

glory and worship. Giving glory to God is worshipping Him. The glory we give to God can never be more than worship. Bowing before Him is the worship He receives from us. Worship is being able to bow before God and say to Him, "I submit to You." The proud cannot worship God. Proud people can never worship God because when their way is prosperous, they attribute it to their own ability or to chance. They say, "I was smart to do this or to say this." They think, "I was lucky to meet this person." This kind of person can never give glory to God because He does not worship God. Being a true worshipper of God is offering praise and thanksgiving to Him for everything He has done for us and everything He has given us along the way. Let me say that many times we will not be able to refrain from bowing down and giving glory to God. We will have no other choice but to say, "God, I worship You."

When Abraham's servant went with Rebekah to her house, he explained his mission to Laban, Bethuel, and the rest of her family and told them that he wanted to take Rebekah back with him (Gen. 24:34-49). When Laban and Bethuel heard his story, they acknowledged Jehovah and let Rebekah go (vv. 50-51). We might say that he was very lucky or that he was very shrewd because the matter prospered so well. If we say this, however, it shows that we do not know God, nor have we seen Him. But here was a person who knew God and saw His acts. He had a special trait. Even when his way was prospered to such an extent, he did not rejoice or thank those he was with, he just bowed down to the earth unto the Lord (v. 52). This is real worship.

Brothers and sisters, we must learn to recognize God's ways. I do not know how to press this truth home, but I would reiterate that we need to know two matters. We have two roads. After becoming Christians, we must learn to know the will of God and the work of God on the one hand, and we must learn to know the ways of God, the methods by which He deals with us on the other hand. We must worship God, and we also must accept the ways in which He deals with us. The journey of Abraham's old servant was very prosperous, but he had an outstanding characteristic: His reaction to everything he met was to immediately worship Jehovah.

We have said before and we will say again that if we really want to worship God, we will find again and again that He gives us many opportunities to worship Him. When the old servant arrived at the gate of the village, he worshipped God, and he worshipped again at the door of Laban's home. When he got inside, he worshipped yet again. When we worship God the first time, He will give us a second opportunity to worship Him. God will do one thing to cause us to worship in speechless wonder. Then He will do something else for which we cannot help but worship Him. Many times God will give us a prosperous way. In these times, we must confess that it is not by our own hand or ordination. It did not happen because we are capable, but because Jehovah did it all. Jehovah led us; therefore, all the glory should go to Him.

Worshipping God
for Looking upon Our Afflictions

Our second illustration is found in Exodus 4, when God sent Moses to tell the children of Israel that He had visited them and would deliver them out of the bondage of Egypt. They would not have to fire bricks, the material used to build the tower of Babel. Verse 31 says, "And when [the people] heard that the Lord had visited the children of Israel, and that he had looked upon their affliction, then they bowed their heads and worshipped." Do we have a group of people worshipping God for His ways? Many times it seems as if God is leading us in just the same way as He led Abraham's servant. When our way is well-prospered, we cannot but worship God. Here, however, the situation is different. They worshipped here because God visited them and looked upon their affliction. God did nothing but tell the children of Israel through Moses and Aaron that He had remembered them despite the passage of four hundred thirty years. God had visited them and looked upon their affliction. The meaning of *looked* is "saw." God saw what happened to them. When the Israelites saw that God remembered, visited, and looked upon them, they bowed their heads and worshipped.

Many times our brothers and sisters suffer trials. They cannot worship God because they think God has forgotten them. Many people have domestic difficulties, but the difficulties never last for four hundred thirty years. How can we say that God has forgotten us? Perhaps the children of Israel said, "We have been slaves for so many years, God does not care," just as we may say, "I have been sick for so long, God would not heal me. I have been unemployed for years, but God will not make a way for me. My husband still does not believe; there are still problems in my family." It seems that God has forgotten us, our difficulties, and our sufferings. But if we say these things, our lips will be sealed and we will not worship God. We will have no way to offer a word of worship to God. But a day will come when we see God. We will know Him and understand His ways, and we will see that God has not forgotten our situation. We will tell God that everything we went through was for our benefit; we will bow our head to say, "God, I worship You." We will be unable to refrain from worshipping God because of our gratitude. We will say, "God, I worship You for all the grace and blessings You have given me."

Worshipping God for His Salvation

In Exodus 12:27 God commanded the Israelites to teach their children about the meaning of the Passover: "It is the sacrifice of the Lord's passover, who passed over the houses of the children of Israel in Egypt, when he smote the Egyptians, and delivered our houses." How did the Israelites receive this message? "The people bowed the head and worshipped." The people worshipped God. Please remember that in the Old Testament the sacrifice of the Passover was not a sin offering but a memorial sacrifice. This memorial sacrifice caused the people to worship God. God destroyed the firstborn in all the houses of the Egyptians, but He passed over all the houses of the children of Israel. As they recalled the separation that God had made between His people and the worldly people and the different places to which each had been brought, they could not help but worship Him.

The Passover, like our Lord's table meeting, is a memorial sacrifice and feast to recall the Lord's work and our separation from the world, the recollection of which begets worship in our hearts. We wonder why God ever chose us! We are constrained to worship because of God's way in His selection. Many times God's grace only causes us to give thanks, but it cannot cause us to worship. When we see God's ways, however, we cannot refrain from worshipping. When the Israelites saw the ways of God, they seemingly could not help but say, "God, there are so many people in Egypt, why would You pass over the houses of Israel and strike the houses of the Egyptians? Every firstborn of the Egyptians was slain; how could the first-born of the Israelites be spared? God, how did You do this?" When we see what God has done and how He has chosen us, we will worship Him. The methods by which God does things are His ways. God not only gives grace to us, but the ways in which He gives grace and chooses us cause us to worship God.

Have we thought about these matters? I often think about the time when I was saved as a student. There were more than four hundred other students in the school. God did not choose any of those other students. Why would He choose me? My father had twelve brothers and sisters. Among such a tribe, God did not choose another; He chose me. When we think of the way in which God chose us, we are not just thinking of the grace of God. We do not just give thanks; we also worship God for the way in which He works. Worshipping is acknowledging that God has given grace in such a way. This is not just a matter of God giving grace, but of the way in which grace is given. Since He has given grace in such a way, we should say, "God, I worship You. These are Your ways. You are God."

O brothers and sisters, these are the ways of God! We might ask why He saved us. Let me say that He saved us because it was His delight to choose us. He wanted this and ordained this. There is nothing for us to say. We can only bow our head and fall before Him, saying, "God, I worship You. You not only have grace, but also You take wonderful ways to dispense Your grace." The children of Israel did not merely give thanks to God upon seeing this; they also worshipped Him.

At the breaking of the bread, as we contemplate His grace in saving, justifying, and regenerating sinners like ourselves, and in making us become His children, we offer thanks to God. But when we think of the way in which He forgave our sins, the process He went through to justify us, and the pains He took to pull us out of the muck and mire from among the thousands of other people around us, and when we think of how we happened to be in a certain church and happened to hear a particular gospel message preached by just the right person, and how that enabled us to receive Him, we remember God's ways. We will offer not only thanks but also worship. We will worship the God who orders our way. When we know the ways of God, we cannot refrain from worshipping Him.

There is a marvelous point in this verse. When the children of Israel heard the word, they bowed their heads and worshipped. Moses did not teach them this; Moses did not tell them that they should worship. He just spoke the word of God to them, and they simply worshipped. Worship does not require instruction, exhortation, or mental exercise. When we see the ways of God, we spontaneously worship Him.

Worshipping God
at the Proclamation of His Ways

In Exodus 32—34 we read of a serious difficulty that Moses encountered. God gave him two tablets of stone with the Ten Commandments written on them. While

Moses was still on the mountain, trouble broke out among the Israelites at the foot of the mount. The people made a golden calf and worshipped it. This provoked God to great displeasure and He said to Moses: "Go, get thee down; for thy people, which thou broughtest up out of the land of Egypt, have corrupted themselves: they have turned aside quickly out of the way which I commanded them: they have made them a molten calf, and have worshipped it, and have sacrificed thereunto, and said, These be thy gods, O Israel, which have brought thee up out of the land of Egypt. And the Lord said unto Moses, I have seen this people, and behold, it is a stiffnecked people: now therefore let me alone, that my wrath may wax hot against them, and that I may consume them: and I will make of thee a great nation" (32:7-10). God was furious, so Moses pleaded with God on the one hand and went down the mountain to deal with matters on the other. Thereafter, he ascended the mountain again and in obedience to God's command hewed two more tablets of stone. With these in his hand, he went to the top of Mount Sinai. There God made a solemn proclamation. First He said, "The Lord, The Lord God, merciful and gracious, long-suffering, and abundant in goodness and truth, keeping mercy for thousands, forgiving iniquity and transgression and sin" (34:6-7). If at this point Moses had fallen down and worshipped God, it would not have been surprising; but what is amazing is that he made haste to do so after the second part of the proclamation. The second part was totally different from the first. The first part spoke of God's compassion, grace, mercy, and forgiveness, but in the second part He said, "And that will by no means clear the guilty; visiting the iniquity of the fathers upon the children, and upon the children's children, unto the third and to the fourth generation." When God had proclaimed the awe of His majesty, "Moses made haste, and bowed his head toward the earth, and worshipped" (v. 8). Please bear in mind that knowing God is not merely a matter of grace. If it were just a matter of grace, it would be all over and there would be no problem, but we need to know God's holiness.

I love verses 8 and 9 in chapter thirty-four. In the latter verse Moses prays, but in the former he worships. He worships and then prays. He acknowledges the rightness of God's ways and then seeks God's grace. He did not say, "You are slow to anger, full of compassion, and ready to forgive, so please have mercy on us and do not do as You plan." We would pray in this way. We always love to pray, "Do not do what You are going to do. Even though this is Your way, do not do it." Moses was very different from us. He took his proper place before God and confessed that God's ways were right. Brothers and sisters, have we ever acknowledged that God's ways are right? Have we ever asked God to do anything that we knew was contrary to His ways of working? Have we ever besought Him to forgive a certain brother and cease to discipline him even when we know that His dealings with that brother were right? If we pray like this, we are not worshipping God. We are, in effect, saying, "O God, please change Your ways. Do not give him a burden, do not let him be sick, do not let him have domestic difficulties." Praying in this way is seeking grace and ignoring the ways of God. In our prayer, we are making ourselves too big; we are not identifying ourselves with God's way. Moses first acknowledged God's authority and His ways. God declared that He would by no means

24

clear the guilty, visiting the iniquity of the fathers upon the children, and upon the children's children, unto the third and to the fourth generation. Moses instantly submitted, saying, "O God, You are right, Your ways are right, and I worship You. Since You have decided to do this and because this is Your way, I can only worship You." Thereafter, he prayed that if he had found grace in God's sight, God would still go up in the midst of His people. He prayed for grace, but only after he had worshipped God.

Sometimes we may visit a brother's home and discover that his child is sick. As we kneel with the husband and wife to pray, we immediately sense that God is not worshipped in this house. We know that God never receives worship in this place. As soon as they kneel in prayer, they say, "O God, heal my child." The first words from their mouths are, "O God, my child must not die; You must heal him." They are telling God what to do. They are deciding God's ways for Him. When they open their mouths, we know that God is not worshipped. I am not saying that we do not know God as our Father. Let me repeat that we need to know God not only as our Father, but as God. It is one thing to be the Father, and it is an entirely different thing to be God. We may visit another brother's home, and again there may be a sick child. When we kneel in prayer with the parents, they pray, "God, we praise You that You are always right. We praise You for allowing our child to become sick. You are never wrong, so we worship You. Everything You do is good. If it pleases You to take the child, we will accept Your will, but if it pleases You to show mercy to us, we ask You to heal him." It is proper to pray, and our worship should not replace our prayer. But we must worship first and then pray. Prayer is saying what I want; worship is acknowledging what God wants. Prayer expresses our desire; worship expresses God's desire. Prayer expresses our will, while worship expresses God's will.

How we need to learn from Moses' actions in Exodus 34:8-9! He saw that God was severe, and he could do nothing but kneel and bow down to the ground. Moses did not reason with God. Moses did not ask Him what would happen if He carried out such a punishment. He did not say, "If You do not forgive their sin, what will the Israelites do? If You visit their iniquity to the third or fourth generation, what will I do? I have led the people in vain. Forty years have passed already; I cannot wait for three or four generations. I am finished. I have worked in vain." Moses did not exhort God to change. Instead, Moses worshipped. I do not know what to say. The greatest need among Christians today is to learn the lesson of knowing God's ways and embracing them. It does not matter how it affects me or what I want. (Moses had a desire. It was a consuming desire of his to enter the land of Canaan.) However, Moses first said, "You are right in whatever You want; I worship You." Brothers and sisters, we must not only learn to do God's will and accept His work; we also need to love God's ways and His decisions. We must like what God likes.

Worshipping God
as the Captain of Jehovah's Army

In the book of Joshua, God commissioned Joshua to lead the Israelites into the land of Canaan. What a weighty responsibility! Moses had become old and died; Aaron had died as well. The only person left was the young man Joshua. Those who had the ability to bear this burden had already gone, leaving a young man alone. What could he do? What must he have felt? The mature, experienced Moses could not do it; how can a young man like himself do it? How could he cope with the seven formidable tribes inhabiting the land of Canaan? And how could he lead a people like the children of Israel with their fear of death and their constant complaints? Joshua was faced with this challenge. Can we blame him for feeling overwhelmed? No, we cannot. If we were in the same circumstances, we would feel overwhelmed too.

At this point, however, Joshua saw a vision of a great Man with a drawn sword. Joshua did not recognize the Man and asked, "Are You for us or for our adversaries?" (5:13). We must pay close attention to this question. How did the Man answer him? Many people erroneously believe that the Man said He had come to help Joshua, but the Man did not answer in this way. In His answer He first said, "Neither," that is, I am not here to help you, nor to help your adversaries. I am here for only one thing; "as the Captain of Jehovah's army

28

have I now come" (v. 14). Thank God for
doing this. Thank God that this is what
the Lord Jesus does! He does not help us,
neither does He help our adversaries, but
He comes as the Captain of the Lord's
army. If we are God's army, then He comes
to be our Captain. This is not a question
of receiving help, but of accepting leadership. He has not come to offer assistance
but to demand subjection. He does not
come to help but to lead. He says, "As the
Captain of Jehovah's army have I now
come." How did Joshua react when he
heard these words? "Joshua fell to the
ground upon his face and worshipped."

Brothers and sisters, we must learn the
ways of God, and this is another of His
ways. God does nothing to assist us or to
assist our enemies. God does not stand in
the midst of the conflict giving a little help
here or there. God wants to be the Captain,
and He demands our submission. In the
face of so many foes, the need would not
be answered if God merely helped us.
Submitting to Him will solve the whole
problem.

The issue is not whether or not God is
helping us, but whether we are submitting to His leadership. When He is in

command, all is well. A great trouble today among God's children is that we want everything to revolve around us and everything to serve our interests. But God will not allow this. He wants to bring us to the point of simply submitting to Him. When this matter is settled, all other problems vanish.

Joshua fell to the ground upon his face and worshipped. If we know God's ways by knowing Him as our Captain, God will handle everything, and we will worship Him. God does not come to assist us in battle; He comes to lead the troops. If we hope He will help us in the fight, we have misunderstood God. God comes to lead the troops. We must submit before Him. When we learn the true meaning of worship, we will also know that there is now a sword drawn on our behalf.

Worshipping God
for Opening the Way

In the book of Judges there is a section that relates to Gideon. In chapter seven Gideon had no assurance; he did not know if he would be able to win the battle. He went to the camp of the Midianites and heard one Midianite say to another, "I have just had a dream. There was this round loaf of barley bread tumbling through the camp of Midian. And it came to the tent and struck it, so that it fell and turned upside down. And the tent collapsed. And his companion answered and said, This is nothing else but the sword of Gideon the son of Joash, a man of Israel. God has delivered Midian and all the camp into his hand." When Gideon heard the account of the dream and its interpretation, he worshipped (vv. 13-15). Gideon did not just worship God; he also worshipped for the things God would do. He did not just worship God for His power; he also worshipped for the way in which God would defeat the Midianites, for His choosing, and for the way in which He was pleased to fight the Midianites. It is God's ways and methods that bring in the worship in this instance. Praise God that it is easy for Him to open a way for us. It seems absurd to expect three hundred men to overthrow the Midianite army, yet God is able to make a way. Please remember that God wants us to constantly emphasize one matter: The portion that God should receive from His children is worship. This does not mean that the work of God is not important, but this does mean that worshipping God is to glorify God. This is what God requires of us.

Worshipping God
for the Gift of a Child

In 1 Samuel 1 we truly touch the spirit of worship. Remember that Hannah did not have any children. Her husband had two wives. The other wife had children, but Hannah was barren and suffered much for it. Therefore, she begged the Lord for a child, and her request was granted. As soon as the child was weaned, she brought him to the temple in Shiloh and said, "It was for this child that I prayed, and Jehovah has granted me my request that I requested from Him. Therefore I, for my part, have lent him to Jehovah; all the days that he lives, he is lent to Jehovah" (vv. 27-28). Do we see these two phrases? They are exceedingly precious to me. Read them together. "Jehovah has granted me... I, for my part, have lent him to Jehovah." Jehovah gave the child to her, and she gave the child back to Him. No answer to prayer surpasses this one. The sum total of her request before God was this child. She had suffered for a lifetime. Her constant hope was to have this child, but what did she say in the end? "What You have given me, I will give to You; I will give You the portion You have given me." O brothers and sisters, of such a person it can be truly written that she "worshipped Jehovah." Hannah worshipped God in this instance. Only the person who wants God Himself, rather than His gift, can worship Him worthily. Hannah showed us what was supremely precious to her—not the gift of God, not the fact He was willing to hear her prayer, not even Samuel whom He gave, but God's way in giving Samuel to her.

God gave her Samuel, so she gave Samuel to God. When Samuel passed out of her hands, worship came forth. Please remember that no one who is not consecrated can worship God. I think that some among us understand this matter. The day in which we give everything to God, including our "Samuel," will be the day in which we begin to learn how to worship. The day in which we see the altar is the day in which we learn to worship.

I can never forget Abraham. Lately, we have referred to him frequently, but I cannot refrain from mentioning him again.

I never cease to be impressed by the preciousness of his remark to his servants in Genesis 22. When he was about to ascend the mountain with Isaac, he said to his servants, "I and the lad will go yonder and worship" (v. 5). He did not say to sacrifice or make an offering, but to worship. It was not sacrifice but worship. His worship was to offer Isaac up to God. It was good for God to do things in this way, and he worshipped Him. O brothers and sisters, I do not believe that anyone who has not really consecrated his all can truly worship God. If we do not have this kind of consecration, we will be unable to worship even if we try. But when the day comes, as it came for Hannah, that our "Samuel," in whom all our hopes are centered, passes out of our hands into God's hands, then worship will flow out to God with him. Hannah knew the ways of God. Since God had given her a son, she gave him to God, not just once, but for all the days of his life. She worshipped God in this position.

Worship always follows the cross and the altar. Wherever there is the cross, the altar, consecration, and obedience to the ways of God, there is worship. Wherever

one gives up working for one's self or
holding on to something for one's self, there
is worship. Worship is saying that we are
not the center. The meaning of worship is
that God is the center. The meaning of
worship is that I step aside and give all
the space to God. It is necessary for
"Samuel" to pass out of our hands.

Worshipping God
for His Vindication of Himself

The ways of God do not always corre-
spond to what we have prayed for. The
reverse is often true. The ways of God do
not always mean prosperity for us; not
infrequently they bring adversity. What
should our attitude be toward these ways
of God? Recall the record of David's sin in
2 Samuel 12. Bathsheba became pregnant
and bore a son. God sent the prophet
Nathan with the message that the child
would surely die. David had sinned, but
he loved his son even though the child was
the fruit of his sin. David, like all fathers,
loved his child. What did he do? He prayed
ceaselessly before God, hoping that God
would heal the child. But God said, "Because you have given the enemies of
Jehovah much occasion to blaspheme Him

because of this thing, the son who is born
to you shall also surely die" (v. 14). You
all know that David knew how to pray. We
can see how well David prayed in the
Psalms. David not only prayed but also
fasted. All night long he lay prostrate on
the ground praying fervently. In the end,
however, the child died.

Anyone who is not consecrated, who
does not know God, who is not truly in
subjection to God, after praying so well
and so fervently with fasting, lying prostrate on the ground all night, surely would
charge God with harshness when such a
request was not granted. Many would say
that God is too strict and would never
worship Him again. They would stop going
to the bread-breaking meeting. They would
stop petitioning God and praying to Him.
Oh, many people have controversy with
God when their ways are not His ways.
They fight and argue with God. They ask
God why He did such a thing to them.
Many people do not submit to God's ways.
They say, "I cannot accept the fact that
You have touched me in this way." They
may not speak this aloud, but they disagree
in their hearts and feel that God is too
harsh.

The strange thing is that when others would have rebelled, David did not rebel. When others would have been disappointed, David was not disappointed. When others would have murmured, David did not murmur. When the child died, his servants were afraid to break the news to him. They thought that if David had been so overwhelmed with anxiety when the child fell sick, his grief would be insupportable when he learned of the child's death. What happened? "Then David rose up from the ground and washed and anointed himself and changed his clothes. And he went to the house of Jehovah and worshipped. Then he went to his house; and when he requested it, they set food before him, and he ate" (v. 20). Worship is bowing to the ways of God. When we submit to the ways of God, this is worship. It is refraining from disappointment and murmuring. It is, henceforth, not being negative, nor arguing with God. Instead, it is saying, "God, You are right in this." This is worshipping God's ways.

It is often necessary for God to do many things to us to vindicate Himself. Do we understand the meaning of this? God often has to vindicate Himself by making it

37

clear to the angels, to the devil, to the world, and to all His children that He has no part in our sin. When we fail, fall, and do certain things, God's governing hand must come in to vindicate Himself by showing all the angels, demons, worldly people, and the church that He has no part in our action. For this reason, God places us in the fire, and His governing hand is upon us; He does not let us off. How do we react at such times? Those who know and love God, those who have a revelation of Him and have seen His appearing, will bow before God and say, "If my suffering vindicates Your holiness, then I say, 'Amen.' If You can make known Your righteousness by my tribulations, then I acknowledge that You do all things well. If Your nature can be vindicated in this way, I gladly accept the sufferings You give me." This is the way to worship God.

Please note that David acted as a normal human being in this experience. I often feel that God's Word shows us people's inner feelings. David was not devoid of love for his child, nor was he lacking in prayer for the boy. He loved his son and prayed for him. He was not devoid of human affections; he was like all other

38

people in the world. Many spiritual people seem to live in an ethereal realm; they do not seem to be living on earth. They do not act like normal human beings but do things in a peculiar manner. In contrast, David was a normal person with human emotions and love. However, when He saw God's ordination in this, he bowed before Him in worship.

May God deliver us from our controversies with Him! We often do not get what we hope, expect, or ask for. If we have the vision, we will say, "God, this is Your way; I bow before You in worship! I know that You are never wrong." Brothers and sisters, let me say again that no one can worship God without submitting to His ways. In order to worship Him, revelation is a basic requirement. In order to worship His ways, subjection is a basic requirement. Apart from revelation, we cannot worship God Himself; apart from subjection we cannot worship His ways. We need to be brought to the point where we say, "God, I submit to You even if You take away what I hold most dear and precious. My submission is worship. You are God; You are never wrong. Your ways are never wrong. I praise You."

I count it as the greatest blessing of my life to have known Miss Barber. Scores of times, perhaps even hundreds of times, I heard her pray, "Lord, I worship You for Your ways." I know these were her deepest, strongest prayers. Scores of times in prayer she said, "God, I praise Your ways." Please remember that God's ways do not always mean a prospering of our ways, nor are they always beneficial to us. God does not always hear our prayer. We may have prayed with fasting, but the child still dies. At this point, we must say, "God I worship you." At such times, we must still worship the ways of God.

Worshipping God for His Stripping

Finally, we need to see that God sometimes refuses prayer because He wants to break us, like breaking David, or wants to vindicate Himself and His holiness. In the following illustration, Job was a righteous man who had herds of cattle, flocks of sheep, and children. One day a servant came to tell him that the Sabeans had stolen all his cattle. Then another servant told him that fire from heaven had burned up all his flocks; nothing was left. Yet another servant told him that he had been robbed and nothing was left. Finally, another servant then came and told him that a great wind from beyond the desert had destroyed his house and killed all his children. Four different servants came and told him that nothing was left (Job 1:13-18). Then Job, whom the Lord said knew of His endurance, rose up, tore his clothes, shaved his head, and fell to the earth and worshipped (v. 20). This was the first thing he did. He not only worshipped God Himself but also His ways. Please remember that there was no element of vindication in this instance as there was in the case of David. It was purely a matter of God doing as He pleased. Nothing was going the right way; there was only suffering. In one day he lost everything; in a matter of minutes he was bereft of everything. Job was a man who submitted to the ways of God. He was able to say, "God, You have done right."

Brothers and sisters, I do not know what you have gone through, but I do know that God is doing a stripping work on many people, causing them to lose much and blocking their ways. I would like to find out how they are reacting. Many people disqualify themselves from blessing because they keep kicking, fighting, and questioning. They murmur, "Why do others not have such difficulties? Why am I the only one with problems? Everyone else turns mud into gold, but I turn gold into mud. Everything I touch goes wrong." They do not understand why it goes well with others while they have problems. It is easy for others to be Christians, but with them it is not so easy. Perhaps they can do things better than others, but they meet with so many difficult situations. Let me say that it does not matter what we say. We still must learn to obey God and submit before Him. We must learn to receive God's ways. God is in our business, among our friends, and in our environment. The ways He has ordained for us are all good. They are good both in suffering and in happiness. When we submit to God's ways, we will worship.

A true worshipper cannot complain. Job 1:20 tells us that we must accept the Lord's ways without question. It does not matter whether the circumstances are good or bad. Practicing this is true worship. I do not know what God's ways are with us. It does not matter whether or not God provides a reason for our suffering; God is always good. God had a reason in David's case; it was his sin. We are able to explain this suffering. However, often there is no reason, no sin. We are not worse than other Christians; we may even be somewhat better than others. So then why do we meet with these difficulties? We should only praise God from the bottom of our hearts and submit to His ways. We must say, "God, what You have done is best. I bow before You in worship because what You have done is best."

May God grant us grace from this day forth to offer Him not only the worship that is borne out of revelation but also the worship that expresses itself in submission and consecration. There are two aspects to our worship; one comes through revelation, and it is the worship of God Himself. The other is to worship the ways of God through our submission. We must say that whatever God does to us is right. Whatever God does is always right.

PRAYER

O God, our God, we want to bow down and worship You. Everything that You have ordained is good. We often choose our own way, but You hinder us and do not prosper us. You seem to cause us to run into a wall. We would like to say that this is best if it pleases You. We cannot ask why You have done this. We cannot ask why You have treated our brothers and sisters in one way and us in another way. We cannot ask why You have given grace to some brothers and sisters but do not give grace to us. We want to accept Your ways. We want to accept them when they are reasonable and when they are not. We want to accept them when they prosper us and when they do not. Teach us to see our ways, and teach us to see Your ways. You do not need to give us a reason for what You have done. Whatever You do is right. Stop us from arguing and reasoning about every matter. Save us from all the "whys." Save us from all the questionings. We look to You to save us. Bring our hearts to the point where we become the footstool to Your throne for You to step. Enable us to submit and to worship. Bless our brothers and sisters. We look to You to give grace to us. In the name of the Lord Jesus, amen.